COLLECTING aRT

A Journal

GLEN HELFAND IN ASSOCIATION WITH GENARTSF

CHRONICLE BOOKS
SAN FRANCISCO

contents

COLLECTING aRT

A Journal

GLEN HELFAND IN ASSOCIATION WITH GENARTSF

GenArtSF's mission is to strengthen and empower the community of young artists, to cultivate a new generation of arts audiences, and to connect the arts community to the community at large.

www.genartsf.org

10 9 8 7 6 5 4 3 2 1

Printed in Hong Kong

Distributed in Canada by
Raincoast Books
9050 Shaughnessy Street
Vancouver, B.C. V6P 6E5

Chronicle Books LLC
85 Second Street
San Francisco, CA 94105
www.chroniclebooks.com

Design by L-B-W, LLC
Photography by Dwight Eschliman

GenArtSF would like to thank the following for their support:
Heather Peeler, Lisa Goodfriend, Gayle Steinbeigle, Katrina Traywick, Fong and Fong Printers and Lithographers, Headlands Center for the Arts, The Painters Place, Holly Blakes, the Board and Founders of GenArtSF, L-B-W, LLC, and Dwight Eschliman

GenArtSF is a project of the San Francisco Community Initiative Funds.

Typeset in Trade Gothic and Bembo

ISBN: 0-8118-3226-0

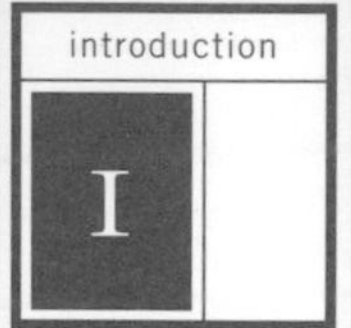
introduction
I

Almost everyone has collected something at one time or another.

It may have been something you spent your hard-earned allowance savings to have or something that nature gives away free. The main thing is that having just one was never enough.

"When I was a kid I was an obsessive collector of PENNIES. *I had every penny imaginable (at least that's how I remember it) and to this day, when I get a penny I get this little twang of excitement that courses through my body—maybe this will be that 1943 Denver mint I've been needing to fill in things. So, I guess in some small way that collection has helped to keep me young at heart."* —*Andrew*

They're objects that have personal associations, memories...

"When I was in boarding school I collected stickers, mostly SCRATCH AND SNIFF STICKERS, *the ones with the googly eyes, and the fluffy ones. One day this girl accused me of stealing her stickers, I got blamed for an act I didn't commit. The head-mistress gave me a demerit. This was fairly traumatic—at the age of eight, I packed up, moved to America, and gave up my sticker collection entirely."* —*Christina*

and family history.

"When I was ten I collected UNICORNS. *By the time my dad caught on, I was no longer into them, but went along with it when he gave me 'uni-gifts.' But then things got out of hand. With a room full of 'uni-gifts' from years past, it got harder and harder to break the news. I'm not sure that I ever did. I hope he's not reading this."* —*Diane*

And as you got older, perhaps the object of your collecting affection may have grown more adult:

"My collection of MARTINI SHAKERS *numbers about 30—from the sleek art deco cobalt blue to the tacky 50's theme of hillbillies swigging jugs. I love how while you sip your drink you can also savor the clean, cool design of your shaker. Usually that includes taking in designs inspired by the most outrageous imagery of American life. The last shaker that entered my collection took the longest to find. The dancing pink elephant motif haunted me day and night until one fateful afternoon in Southern California when I found an elephant shaker on a dusty shelf in a dingy junk shop. I celebrated by changing my drink of choice and mixed up a shaker of pink Cosmopolitans!" —Didi*

Those things may be reflections of your past (or someone else's)...

"I like BAUER BOWLS *because they're old and have history—they belonged to someone else. I collect shades of* BLUE *and* GREEN *because those colors remind me of Miles Davis's music. They all give me a good feeling, a little bit of sky and a little bit of ground." —Suzi*

or perhaps your everyday reality.

"I collect EVERYTHING*—which is to say I throw away nothing. I search for things to add to my piles, as if more of something will shape it into a defined collection. I won't even throw my clothes away because I think they could make good costumes someday."* *—Maren*

They're things that are as fun to acquire as they are to display in your living room—or someplace more private.

Acquiring that special object, especially a rare or exquisite example was, and may continue to be, well, an exhilarating experience.

The thrill of art collecting is just that kind of rush. It's exciting to acquire a painting, print, drawing, photograph, or perhaps a new art form that's more difficult to classify. The process of purchasing a work of art is far more involved and complex than your average financial transaction. It takes us into the realm of creativity, self-expression, and personal identity.

There is, however, the perception that art collecting may be a little out of your reach. You may have grown up eagerly anticipating field trips to the art museum, but from an early age, you were taught that those original paintings and sculptures are not exactly things meant for the home. Fine art, you may have been told, is expensive, precious, and definitely not to be touched.

But this is not necessarily the case.

Collectors are similarly characterized as upper crust sorts who have their names etched in polished granite in the lobbies of office buildings and stately arts institutions. Those collectors seem to be part of an elite club that attends exclusive black tie receptions. It's a myth—the art world is a varied place with plenty of more down to earth social gatherings.

Similarly, some contemporary art galleries can resemble the setting for a Woody Allen satire of urban intellectuals, where people discuss elaborate video installations in a language that doesn't sound much like English. Most people, even arts professionals, may find such language confusing—as well as amusing.

There is certainly some truth to the stereotypes (some people even embrace them), but that doesn't mean that there isn't room for the rest of us in the art collector's realm. The art world is really an arena that's as varied as the bounds of creativity, the range of possible styles, and forms of expression.

There's a place there for you, too.

But before you enter confidently, you may need to rethink a few assumptions.

1) Art is not a luxury.

You'll need to accept the fact that visual art fulfills basic human needs for expression and contemplation. It's a process that's been documented back to prehistoric times. Even if you don't own a work of original fine art, you certainly have some form of visual stimulation on your walls, desk or refrigerator door. It could be a postcard someone sent you, a tempera handprint, a snapshot of someone near and dear, a Monet postcard from the Met, or a glossy magazine photograph of your favorite celebrity.

Each of these images visually expresses some kind of personal connection to the world. They're things you've selected from a seemingly endless array of images that everyone encounters daily. Your choices reflect who you are and at the same time provide a little outlet from your daily experiences. To put an original work of art on your wall adds extra layers of meaning to your world, primarily because that piece is something that no one else has.

WHAT DO I OWN THAT EXPRESSES SOMETHING ABOUT ME?

WHAT'S ON MY DESK, REFRIGERATOR DOOR, OR BOOKSHELF THAT HAS PERSONAL MEANING TO ME?

2) An original work doesn't have to be expensive or an investment.

There are collectors who buy undisputed masterpieces for millions of dollars. At that level it may be as much of an investment as an expression of personal taste. But anyone can just as easily spend five bucks on something that might be just as satisfying. Most likely you're buying that work of art that caught your eye not as a way to start a nest egg, but to enhance your life with an object that reflects your own sensibility. And that's a soul-satisfying prospect.

3) Your own taste is as valid as any New York art critic's.

You know what you like, and that's the bottom line. It's okay if you don't go for Picasso's "Blue Period," or don't find conceptual art appealing (though hopefully you'll at least give either a chance). You'll know that a particular painting, sculpture, photograph, collage, or video has to be yours when you just keep thinking about it. That piece should speak to you, inspire you to think in a different way. Sometimes the image will inhabit your dreams. Having it should make you feel enriched and fill you with pleasure. After all, if you do get it, it'll be something you look at on a daily basis. It'll grow more meaningful over time as new thoughts and associations emerge.

ARE THERE ANY COMMON CHARACTERISTICS ON MY LIST OF PERSONAL OBJECTS? WHAT ARE THEY?

4) The gallery is not the only place to find artwork.

These days, art museums are shifting their profiles for a new century, opening their doors to broader audiences and finding ways to make exhibitions more user-friendly. Art shows are frequently becoming the topic of daily conversation, and the idea of art in general is becoming more approachable. The Internet is also bringing artwork directly to the people. Cyberspace is filled with online galleries (where you'll never have to worry about how to dress for a visit), as well as numerous e-auction houses and guides to finding out when artists open their studios to the public for a bit of direct interaction with the public.

WHEN AND WHERE DID I FIND THE OBJECTS ON MY LIST?

WHAT DO I REMEMBER ABOUT GETTING THEM?

WHAT MEANING DO THEY HOLD FOR ME?

DO THEY REMIND ME OF ANYTHING OR ANYONE?

The purpose of this journal

is to ease you into the process so you can get out there and find that piece that will fuel your passion to collect.

There's a lot to consider, but diving in can be a lot of

fun.

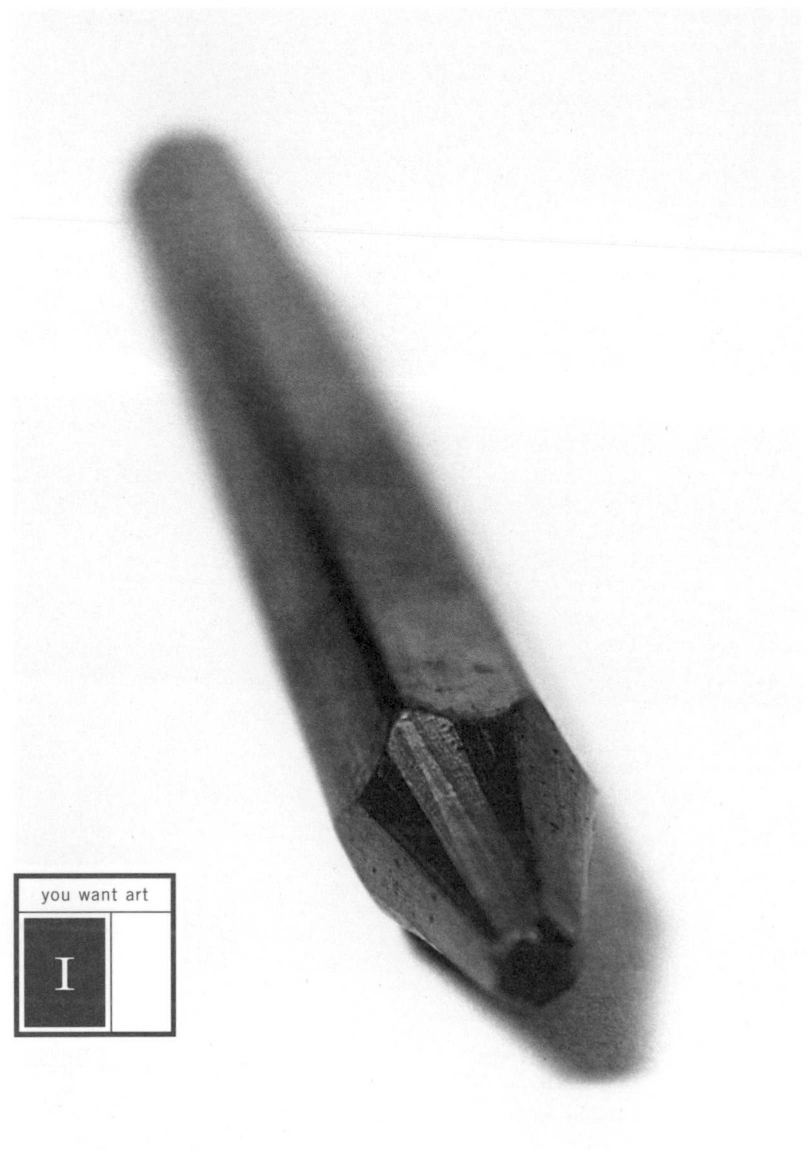

I

you want art

you want

I don't know a lot about art, but I know what I like.

It's a stand-up comedy line, but has a lot more credence than you might expect. Chances are, you really do know what you like, but the critical language that often circulates around the fine arts may give you cause for wonder. Don't worry—those impenetrable reviews are most likely the art world equivalent of a trade magazine, filled with technical terms that you don't necessarily need to know.

You don't often question why you adore sipping a certain Chardonnay, savoring a California roll from your favorite sushi bar, or devouring a big bag of popcorn while watching a sitcom. You shouldn't second-guess your own tastes when it comes to art either. The possibilities are infinite, and what you choose, and the efforts you make to obtain those things, is an expression of your tastes. You know what you like.

There are images and objects you gravitate towards and enjoy experiencing, without necessarily knowing why. There is no reason to doubt those instincts, but why not investigate them?

MY FAVORITE COLOR IS

MY FAVORITE FLOWER IS

MY FAVORITE MOVIE IS

MY FAVORITE KIND OF MUSIC IS

MY FAVORITE CONDIMENT IS

WHAT DO MY FAVORITES SAY ABOUT ME?

Art calls for introspection. There's something there that makes you sit in front of a favorite painting every time you go to the museum or linger over and perhaps clip out a particular photograph in a book or magazine. There's a dynamic between that image or object and yourself. The art piece you'll buy is something you'll experience repeatedly—it's worth considering why it speaks to you, and how long it might continue to do so. Is this something you'll want to look at every day or will you tire of it?

Art collecting also requires a bit of an investment. A painting may cost more than cheese puffs (but not necessarily more than a very good bottle of wine), so there are more things to consider before making a purchase. We'll discuss them later in these pages.

MY FAVORITE PIECES OF ART, POSTERS, OR PRINTS IN MY HOME RIGHT NOW ARE

WHAT ABOUT THEM DO I FIND APPEALING?

WHAT DO THEY SAY ABOUT MY LIKES OR DISLIKES?

I WOULD DESCRIBE MY TASTE AS

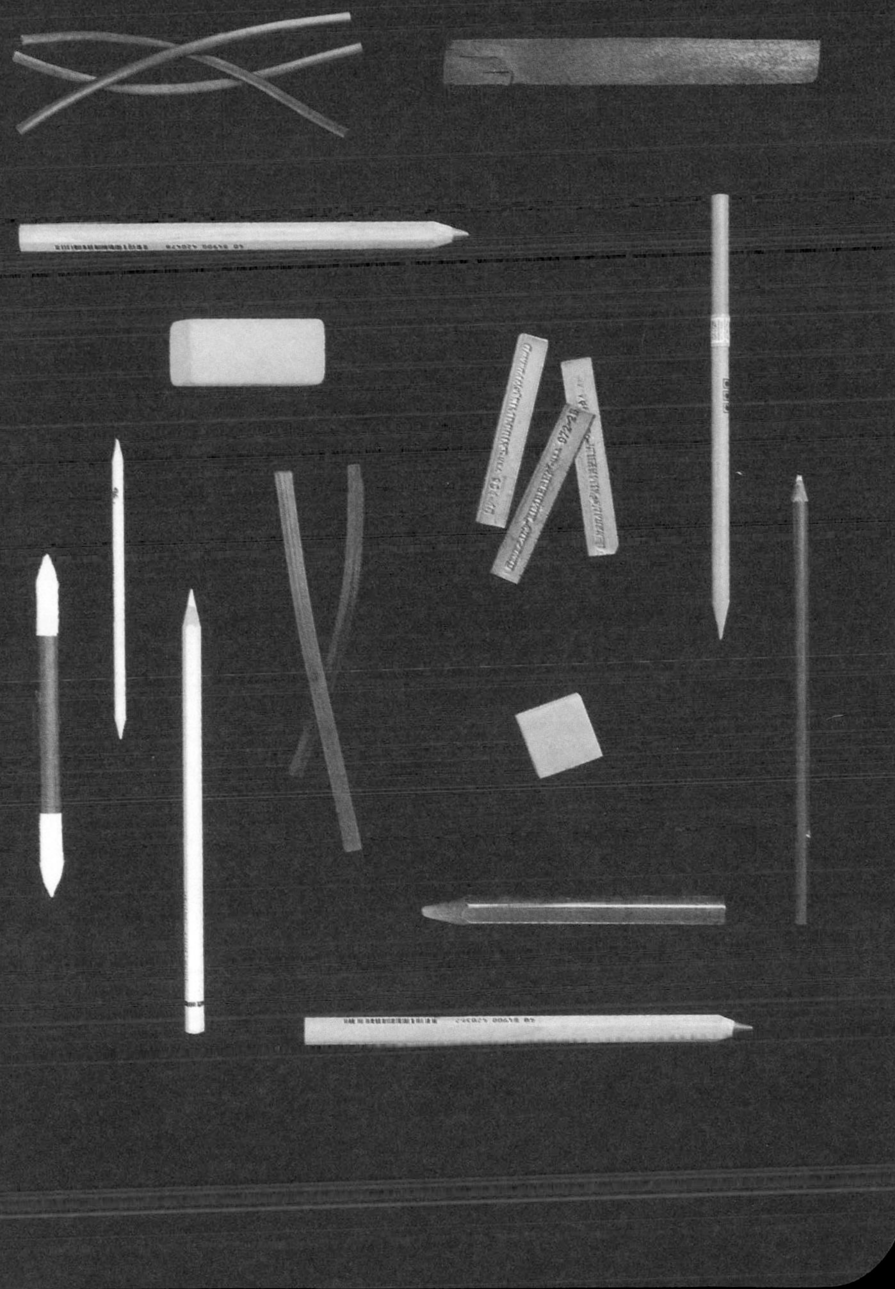

art is accessible

2

aRT

is accessible

But, you ask, how and where do I begin?

First, open your eyes and really

look

Where? Well, there are many different types of venues in which to see art.

A work of art is something to build a relationship with. Get to know it before you make a commitment.

Museums

Make regular visits to museums and stroll through their permanent collections and special exhibitions. (Consider buying a membership to support the institution and save some money, too.) As you look, keep your eyes and mind open and see where you end up. Are you attracted to realistic landscape paintings, abstract drawings composed of carefully ordered lines, or soft-focus black-and-white photographs? If there are pieces you really like, make a note not only of the artists' names, but also of the qualities that attract you to their work. Is it the color, the texture, the scale, or the subject matter? Don't worry, the criteria aren't important, you're just gathering information. You might also make note of what you don't like. If something sparks a highly negative response, that tells you something, too.

Have fun and check things out. Afterwards, you can always sit at the museum café and people watch as you review your notes and think about what you've seen.

THE FIRST ART MUSEUM I REMEMBER VISITING WAS

I SAW

I LIKED

I DISLIKED

THE LAST TIME I WENT TO AN ART MUSEUM WAS

MY IMPRESSIONS OF THE PLACE, ITS ATMOSPHERE, ARCHITECTURE, AND FELLOW VISITORS WERE

WHICH PAINTINGS, SCULPTURES, OR PHOTOGRAPHS CAUGHT MY EYE RIGHT AWAY?

WHAT ABOUT THEM DREW ME IN?

HOW LONG DID I LOOK AT THEM?

Galleries

Next you'll want to visit some art galleries. The best strategy is to have two or three specific destinations in mind. Pick up a gallery guide, look in the newspaper, or go online to help plan your outing.

Once there, take the time to really look at the work—whether you like what you see or not.

There are several different types of galleries: commercial (or retail), non-profit or not-for-profit, and alternative spaces. Simply put, commercial galleries sell art for a profit (the gallery typically splits the sale price 50/50 with the artist.) The galleries you encounter in shopping malls or tourist areas tend to be more commercial and often employ high-pressure sales tactics. These are usually avoided by more seasoned collectors.

Non-profit or alternative spaces may or may not sell the works of art on display. The funding for these galleries comes from private, corporate, and/or government sources. Typically, more established (and higher priced) artists show at commercial spaces while younger, emerging artists get their start at alternative spaces.

Let's start with commercial spaces, which often are grouped in a single art-intensive district or building, making it easier to compare and contrast the offerings at each. If you feel a bit hesitant to enter into those sometimes intimidating white-walled establishments, go with friends, or attend an opening reception when there are more people around, and complimentary glasses of Chardonnay. Most cities have a number of art openings the same evening every month—you can become part of the art community that attends these events, thus expanding your circle of knowledge, contacts, and art collecting peers. Sometimes there are organized gallery walks or art fairs—again check out the art listings in the alternative weekly newspapers or gallery guides. These are good events that allow you to get your feet wet.

On your way out of the gallery, sign their mailing list so you'll get announcements of upcoming exhibitions. While you look at the shows, practice the same note-taking process you began in the museum.

LIST OF GALLERIES I HAVE VISITED:

THE GALLERIES I FELT MOST COMFORTABLE IN WERE

WHY?

ANY PARTICULAR PIECES THAT I LOVED?

WHAT ABOUT THEM WAS SO APPEALING?

PARTICULAR ARTISTS I LIKED OR FOUND INTERESTING WERE

Non-Profit/Alternative Galleries

To get a more inside view of the visual arts, you'll want to investigate the realm of alternative and non-profit galleries.

These are exhibition spaces where the emphasis is on artistic expression rather than sales. They can be publicly funded, city supported, run by collectors, patrons, or scrappy artist collectives. The shows tend to be more adventurous, ephemeral, or experimental in nature, and concentrate on younger and emerging, just-out-of-art school artists, who are given a career-building showcase for their developing work. Not surprisingly, the audiences at alternative spaces are artists themselves and are very much reflections of the local creative community. Though they might be termed non-profit spaces, you can always inquire about purchasing something.

WHAT ALTERNATIVE GALLERIES HAVE I VISITED?

DID I NOTICE ANY DIFFERENCE BETWEEN THEM AND THE COMMERCIAL GALLERIES I'VE BEEN TO?

ANY PARTICULAR PIECES THAT I LOVED?

WHAT WAS SO APPEALING ABOUT THEM?

PARTICULAR ARTISTS I LIKED OR FOUND INTERESTING WERE

Read/Learn

In addition to gathering some first-hand experience, read up on the subject of art.

Immerse yourself in art. Learn its language.

Peruse the newsstand and flip through those domestic and international glossy art magazines. (A list can be found in the Resources section.) They too have their own sense of tone and style—some are more theoretical, others more commercial-oriented. Many offer a straightforward look at art activity across the nation (with a bit of juicy art world gossip thrown in for good measure) while other publications have a more insider edge and address film, fashion, and technology from an art world perspective. There are also a number of periodicals devoted to specific types of art, like sculpture or printmaking.

Pay attention to what grabs you in those pages. Read art reviews. The critic's word is not the final say on any object, but reading art criticism is a great way to become familiar with art names and terms, and to learn how art is discussed and assessed. (Check out the recommended titles in the Resources section.) There are, of course, endless numbers of books available as well. Go to the library or your favorite bookstore and spend time browsing through artist monographs, which are deluxe books devoted to a single artist, and exhibition catalogs, which function as a supplement to and record of a museum or gallery show.

Sign for up for a class—perhaps a survey of art history or a more focused course. Attend lectures, seminars, and events.

Check out the big new museums when traveling—you could plan a great trip around one of the newer, high-profile institutions: Frank Gehry's Guggenheim in Bilbao, Spain; the Getty Center designed by Richard Meier in Los Angeles; the Tate Modern by Herzog + de Meuron in London. You'll discover a whole new world (and get a little architectural history thrown in with your art appreciation).

AT THE BOOKSTORE, WHICH TITLES ON THE ART BOOK TABLE CAUGHT MY EYE?

WHY?

WHICH ART MAGAZINES DID I FLIP THROUGH?

WHAT WAS MY IMPRESSION OF THESE PUBLICATIONS AND THE ART INSIDE THEM?

I WANTED TO BUY

I BOUGHT

Read/Learn

"I once owned a Roy Lichtenstein print that I foolishly sold. When I realized I wanted it back, I went searching for it online, and found one pretty quickly. It was kind of amazing." —George

In the same way that digital technology has reshaped most every aspect of contemporary life, the Web has added new options to the process of art collecting. It has brought this once rarified practice directly and intimately to our personal computers, and created more ways in which to entertain the prospect of art collecting.

Use the Web as a resource to learn more about an artist you were intrigued by in a magazine or gallery. Through your favorite search engine you'll find reviews, resumes, and perhaps even works for sale. There are numerous Web sites that sell and/or auction art the electronic way, and the volume of cyberspace allows them to showcase considerably more artwork than a bricks and mortar gallery can.

The process of finding the right online source is similar to selecting a real-world dealer—browse and see if the site reflects your aesthetic interests and sensibilities. The beauty is you can do it during off-hours, in your PJs. And you can avoid the intimidation factor that can sometimes accompany a trip to an actual gallery. If you buy from an online source, works will be shipped to you, carefully packaged (sometimes at an additional cost). You can do all your consulting and purchases via e-mail.

Some sites follow a gallery model, offering original works by hundreds of contemporary artists and craftspeople, both emerging and established, at modest prices, from a few hundred dollars to a few thousand. Like most art sites, they highlight works in various fashions—online exhibitions, sections devoted to media, subject or affordability—as well as make objects available through sophisticated search engines. They also include sections with art collecting tips.

Other art sites group together a number of real world galleries, e-shopping mall-style, and make their work available online. Traditionally, when you consult with an out-of-town gallery, slides or transparencies of artwork are sent by mail. This type of site uses the Web's quick delivery capabilities to get images to prospective collectors quickly and inexpensively. Yet another online gallery model works directly with artists to create limited edition prints, photographs, sculptures, or other objects.

Finally, auction sites, be they born on the Web or the online offshoot of a time-honored house, have plenty of art available from private individuals or dealers. These are offered singly, making an online auction purchase more suited to those who know exactly what they're looking for.

Online sellers boast quantity and convenience. The main thing to be aware of in this arena is that the Web is a representational medium; you won't experience an artwork's sense of scale or texture here. Online art sellers are well aware of this fact, and usually have easy return policies. If you've done your homework, an online site can be a perfect vehicle to acquire art.

WHICH GALLERY OR MUSEUM SITES HAVE I LOOKED AT ONLINE?

I NOTICED

ANY ART THAT I PARTICULARLY LOVED?

WHY?

HOW WOULD I COMPARE LOOKING AT ART ONLINE TO SEEING IT IN A MUSEUM OR GALLERY?

You might want to note some specific things you've found in each of the art venues in the pages that follow.

THE FOLLOWING GALLERIES OR MUSEUM SHOWS HAVE INSPIRED ME TO COLLECT

WHAT ABOUT THEM EXCITED ME?

I FOUND THE FOLLOWING ARTISTS APPEALING

I CAN FIND THEIR WORK AT

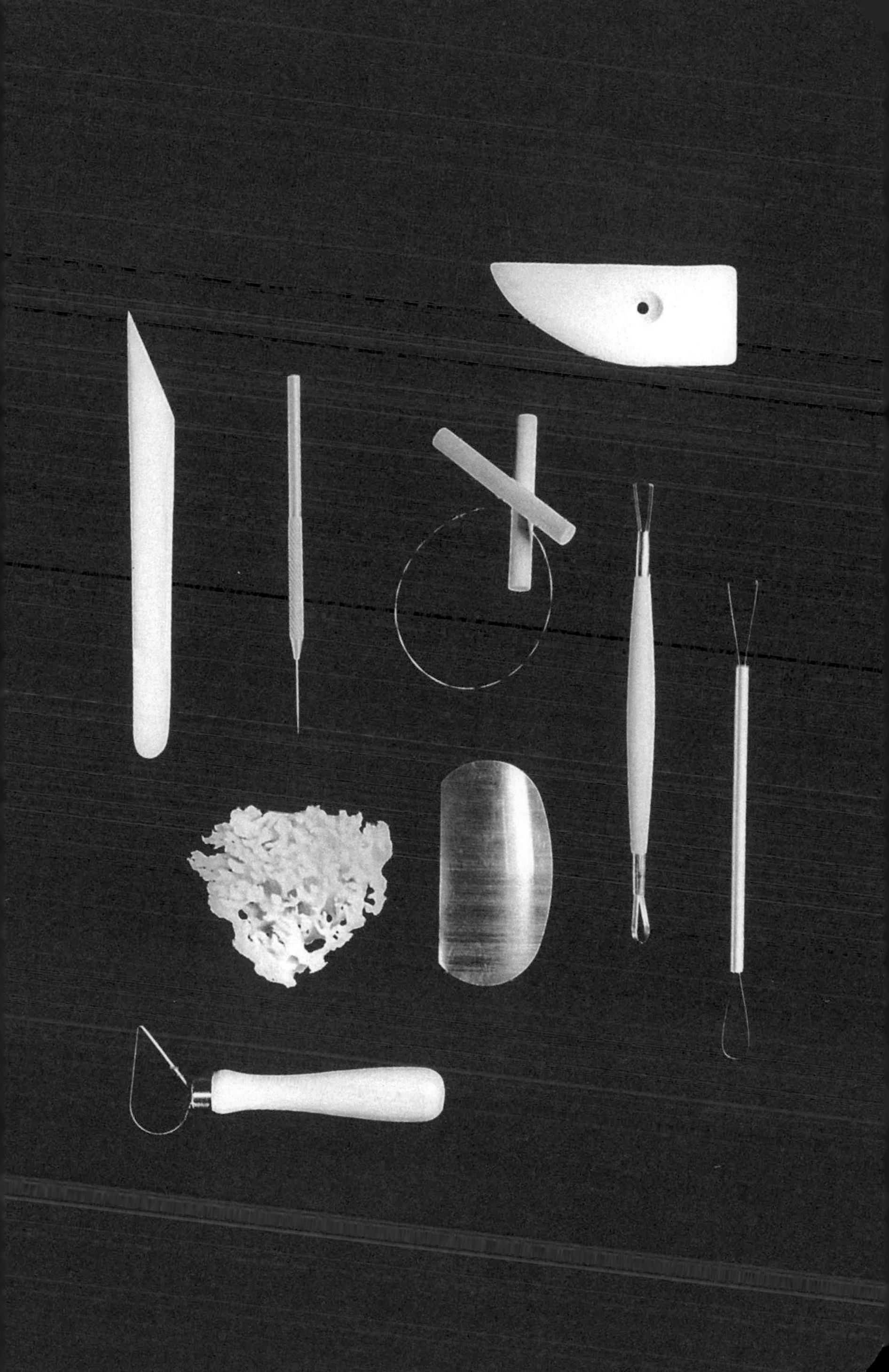

choosing art

3

choosing aRT

"A few years ago I went to a gallery and saw this carved wood sculpture of Spiderman, my favorite superhero, doing something sort of naughty. I immediately fell in love with it. Though I'd never spent that much on art before, the thought of having it was too good to pass up. I went back to the gallery and worked out a deal. It's been a few years and I still love seeing it every day. It was the beginning of my collection of carved wood sculpture, which now includes about twenty pieces." —Michael

So you're seeing and
interacting with art.

As you start to notice what pieces you are attracted to, it's worth becoming more familiar with the different media, materials, and techniques. In this way, you'll be able to get a better sense of what constitutes good craftsmanship or where artwork fits in the continuum of art history.

Each medium or technique is consciously chosen by artists to achieve various aesthetic ends. And each has a different quality when it comes to considerations of display and ownership, and why you might be attracted to it.

Painting

When the word art comes up in general conversation, chances are it's in reference to painting—the kingpin of art media.

In dictionary terms, painting is, simply, an aesthetic entity created by the skilled covering of a surface with paint. The range of possibilities within those parameters, however, is seemingly limitless. The type of paint and surface can create strikingly different effects. Oil on canvas is the classic form—the Mona Lisa is one example, but there are plenty of alternatives—and they don't always include what we traditionally consider paint. In the pigment category there's acrylic, watercolor, gouache, latex house paint, a wax-like substance called encaustic and various liquids such as coffee, grape juice, and the like. These can be applied to any manner of surface, from linen, wood panel, glass, gauze, TV trays, old suitcases, and so on. They can be mixed and matched at will. Some, oil and acrylic, can form a thick, textured brushstroke called impasto, while others are thinner fluids that create flatter, more graphic effects. Watercolor is such a medium. Painting is usually, but not always, two-dimensional. Most likely you can hang one on your wall, but a painting can also be created directly on the wall as a mural.

WHAT FAMOUS PAINTINGS HAVE I ALWAYS ADMIRED?

WHAT ATTRACTS ME TO THEM?

ARE THEY ABSTRACT OR REPRESENTATIONAL?

WHAT KINDS OF PAINTING STYLES OR TECHNIQUES DO I RESPOND TO MOST?

WHY?

THE FIRST PAINTING I BOUGHT (OR WANTED TO) WAS

THE ARTIST'S NAME WAS

WHERE AND WHEN I SAW/BOUGHT IT

IT COST

Drawing

You can safely define a drawing as a conglomeration of marks that adds up to something much more.

In the most traditional sense, drawings are graphite pencil, charcoal, or pastel on a sturdy quality paper. Sometimes they're sketches for a painting or sculpture by an Old Master or a cartoon-like character by Keith Haring. A drawing can also be a finished product in its own right. The fairly simple means make this a medium that often allows for more spontaneous expression than painting. But that doesn't mean they're always carefree doodles on a café napkin (though one dashed off by Picasso, or another such accomplished artist, is certainly of value). A number of artists create drawings that are labor intensive, be they representations of realistic subjects or finely detailed abstractions composed of thousands of lines. Generally, this is an intimate medium—drawings tend to be smallish in scale and more affordable than paintings.

The media, methods, and surfaces used in drawing can take interesting and unexpected turns—in the realm of art there are no hard and fast rules.

A drawing can be created with unexpectedly simple means on an unlikely surface—etched into glass, for example, or Bic pen on old funny pages from the Sunday paper. Whatever the material, drawings can be delicate. Paper tends to be sensitive to light, so you'll want to find out if it's archival, that is, if the surface is made to withstand the tests of time. You'll also need to consider framing it under protective glass or displaying it someplace that doesn't get direct exposure to the sun.

WHAT FAMOUS DRAWINGS HAVE I ALWAYS ADMIRED?

WHAT ATTRACTS ME TO THEM?

ARE THEY ABSTRACT OR REPRESENTATIONAL?

WHAT KINDS OF DRAWING STYLES OR TECHNIQUES DO I RESPOND TO MOST?

WHY?

THE FIRST DRAWING I BOUGHT (OR WANTED TO) WAS

THE ARTIST'S NAME WAS

WHERE AND WHEN I SAW/BOUGHT IT

IT COST

Prints

A close relative to drawings, fine art prints are works that employ a number of processes that transfer an image from one surface—a printing plate—to another, usually paper.

The prints can be made multiple times, and the number of prints made from a particular plate is called the edition, i.e. "an edition of 25". There are various types of prints—etchings, silkscreen, lithography and linocut (remember those potato prints you made in nursery school?) among them—and each time-honored technique has a very different look and feel. Etchings can capture delicate line work (Rembrandt made many etchings), while silkscreen is more suited to larger, more graphic shapes. Silkscreen was, for example, Andy Warhol's favored medium.

Each technique requires special printing presses or other equipment, which is why prints are most often made at businesses which work with artists to develop, produce, and sell the results. Some artists, however, work exclusively with the print medium.

Printmaking is a somewhat specialized realm, with its own terminology, protocol, and price structures. The fewer prints made from a single source, the more valuable they become. Most fine art print editions number less than a hundred. A monoprint is a single print made by applying a one-time composition of paint or ink to a surface. A mass-produced poster is by definition a print, but since there are many copies of it, the value decreases. An artist's proof is a test print that the artist approves as the right mixture of elements before going on to produce the full print run. The proof is generally more affordable than the signed, numbered prints. Since there are more set standards and pricing structures for prints—guidebooks are published listing prices for particular prints—it's a comforting medium for many collectors, and one that can offer more affordable access to big-name artists.

WHAT FAMOUS PRINTS HAVE I ALWAYS ADMIRED?

WHAT ATTRACTS ME TO THEM?

ARE THEY ABSTRACT OR REPRESENTATIONAL?

WHAT KINDS OF DRAWING STYLES OR TECHNIQUES DO I RESPOND TO MOST?

WHY?

THE FIRST PRINT I BOUGHT (OR WANTED TO) WAS

THE ARTIST'S NAME WAS

WHERE AND WHEN I SAW/BOUGHT IT

IT COST

Sculpture

Sculpture is artwork that takes up three-dimensional space. You can walk around it, and experience the object from all its many angles. It will look different from each.

Sculpture inherently deals with physical balance.

A colorful Alexander Calder mobile, for example, is a sculpture that seems buoyant and weightless while actually being a hefty object. A bronze figure by Auguste Rodin, however, may have a sturdy physicality—like a statue in a public square, it's difficult to imagine such a thing being nudged from its perch. Most of us don't have room for such large pieces, but small-scale works should address similar concerns.

A sculpture might be made from sturdy substances like marble, plaster or stone—things used way back in ancient times—to more contemporary materials like inflatable plastics, reflective chrome or rubber recycled from old tires. Scale is also important. You might consider a piece that can fit on your coffee table or book case, or a hardy hunk of stonework that can live in your backyard sculpture garden. If you have kids or pets, you may want to consider whether a specific sculpture would make a viable possession—you wouldn't want the dog to mistake that artist's composition of twigs for a chew toy.

WHAT FAMOUS SCULPTURES HAVE I ALWAYS ADMIRED?

WHAT ATTRACTS ME TO THEM?

ARE THEY ABSTRACT OR REPRESENTATIONAL?

WHAT KINDS OF SCULPTURAL STYLES OR TECHNIQUES DO I RESPOND TO MOST?

WHY?

THE FIRST SCULPTURE I BOUGHT (OR WANTED TO) WAS

THE ARTIST'S NAME WAS

WHERE AND WHEN I SAW/BOUGHT IT

IT COST

Photography

It's a safe bet to assume you've taken a photograph at some point in your life.

Even if it's a snapshot, a Polaroid, or digital picture, it's still the result of photographic technology. For this reason, it's perhaps the most familiar art medium. At the same time, it's one that some still have a difficult time accepting as "art."

When looking at photography in a gallery or museum, you must consider interesting questions, like what are the qualities that make it different than a picture you took with a disposable camera or a documentary image in a newspaper or magazine?

There are many possible distinctions. First might be the vision of the photographer, his or her subject matter, compositional eye, and general sensibility. Ansel Adams made photographs of the beauty of nature while Diane Arbus created austere images of eccentric characters. Each photographer may also have a distinctive printing style. If you've seen one of Adams' black-and-white prints, you've seen what many consider the best of the field, whether he printed on glossy photo paper, which is capable of producing rich tones, or on matte stock, which generates an effect more like a print or work on paper. Many contemporary photographers are creating large, lush color prints that are possible to create using new developments in film and darkroom technologies.

There are different types of prints, which differ because of materials and processes. Gelatin silver or platinum prints are perhaps the most common. Traditional black-and-white photo paper is composed of trace metals suspended in a thin gelatin that hardens when exposed to light. The look of the print varies depending on the type of metal. Color prints are made with different, more complex methods. New digital printing technologies are currently being pioneered, and will introduce whole new mediums to the field.

Since photography is so integrated into our culture, there are many types to collect.

There's a thriving network of dealers who sell vintage photographs—sepia toned images and daguerreotypes from the 19th century, perhaps government sponsored WPA photographs from the 1930s, or any number of photographs from the past. You may be interested in pictures by famous photographers or images by anonymous individuals who may have snapped an incredibly compelling image, by accident or by skill. Some collectors concentrate on documentary photographs while others specialize in specific subjects—interesting images of, say, runners or flowers or the Eiffel Tower. The possibilities are endless.

WHAT FAMOUS PHOTOGRAPHS HAVE I ALWAYS ADMIRED?

WHAT ATTRACTS ME TO THEM?

ARE THEY ABSTRACT OR REPRESENTATIONAL?

WHAT KINDS OF PHOTO STYLES OR TECHNIQUES DO I RESPOND TO MOST?

WHY?

THE FIRST PHOTOGRAPH I BOUGHT (OR WANTED TO) WAS

THE ARTIST'S NAME WAS

WHERE AND WHEN I SAW/BOUGHT IT

IT COST

Installation Art

In the realm of contemporary art, the installation can be something of a catchall medium.

It's something composed of a variety of things, a combination of two- and three-dimensional work. It could be an environment composed of, say, paintings on the walls and a related sculpture. The American artist Ann Hamilton, for example, has made art pieces composed of thousands of shiny copper pennies piled in the center of a room. But an installation can be a more simple and subtle use of lighting or painting words on the wall—like the work of conceptual artist Lawrence Weiner.

The term installation stems from the notions of things installed. It requires a greater sense of adventurousness and commitment from collectors than other types of art as it usually requires a larger amount of space and sometimes more maintenance. The artists take a more active role as they most often install the art themselves, creating a more interactive relationship with the collector.

WHAT INSTALLATIONS HAVE I FOUND MEMORABLE IN MUSEUM OR GALLERY SHOWS?

WHAT ATTRACTED ME TO THEM?

PROS AND CONS (AND FEASIBILITY) OF OWNING AN INSTALLATION:

New Media

Living in a technological age, you're faced with innovative new things almost daily.

The same things that go into creating computers and cell phones often enter the artwork of the current era. New media is the term that applies to forms that veer from the traditional in technological ways. Video art is an early form included in this category. Though it has been in existence since the 1960s, video has only recently been viewed as a viable art form to collect. The situation has been advanced by the popularity of artists like Bill Viola whose video installations have become more prominent in museums and galleries, as have the film and sculpture projects by Matthew Barney. Some artists work with sound as their primary material, recording, perhaps, the sounds of the sea and redirecting them to gallery or public locations. Still others investigate the boundless territory of the World Wide Web, creating projects on the Internet itself. Some forms of new media are more easily collected than others. Video or film projects can be editioned as tapes or DVDs, while sound projects can be sold as CDs. (However, one must consider that playback technologies change rapidly these days.) But true to electronic form, Internet projects are still a big question mark in the realm of collectibility—no one quite knows yet how to "own" them.

DO I FIND VIDEO AND/OR COMPUTER ART APPEALING?

WHY OR WHY NOT?

WHAT'S THE FIRST VIDEO OR COMPUTER PIECE I RECALL SEEING IN A MUSEUM OR GALLERY?

WHAT WAS MEMORABLE ABOUT IT?

WOULD I EVER BUY A PIECE THAT NEEDS TO BE PLUGGED IN?

WHY OR WHY NOT?

You may want to consider checking out your local art school extension program and take a class in any of the aforementioned media so you can really appreciate what goes into making art.

As you collect, you can focus your collection by media, or mix and match. You can buy according to subject, theme, or even type of artist. Your collection can be whatever you want it to be. But it's worth mapping out your goals before you start.

MY GOALS FOR MY COLLECTION ARE

AM I INTERESTED IN COLLECTING ARTWORK IN AN ECLECTIC, IDIOSYNCRATIC MANNER THAT SIMPLY REFLECTS MY TASTE?

DO I WANT TO COLLECT PIECES THAT I THINK WILL HAVE HISTORICAL SIGNIFICANCE?

DO I WANT A LARGE COLLECTION OF INEXPENSIVE WORKS OR A SMALL GROUP OF MORE EXPENSIVE PIECES BY MORE FAMOUS ARTISTS?

DO I WANT MY COLLECTION TO FOCUS ON A PARTICULAR MEDIUM, SUBJECT, OR THEME? WHAT WOULD IT BE?

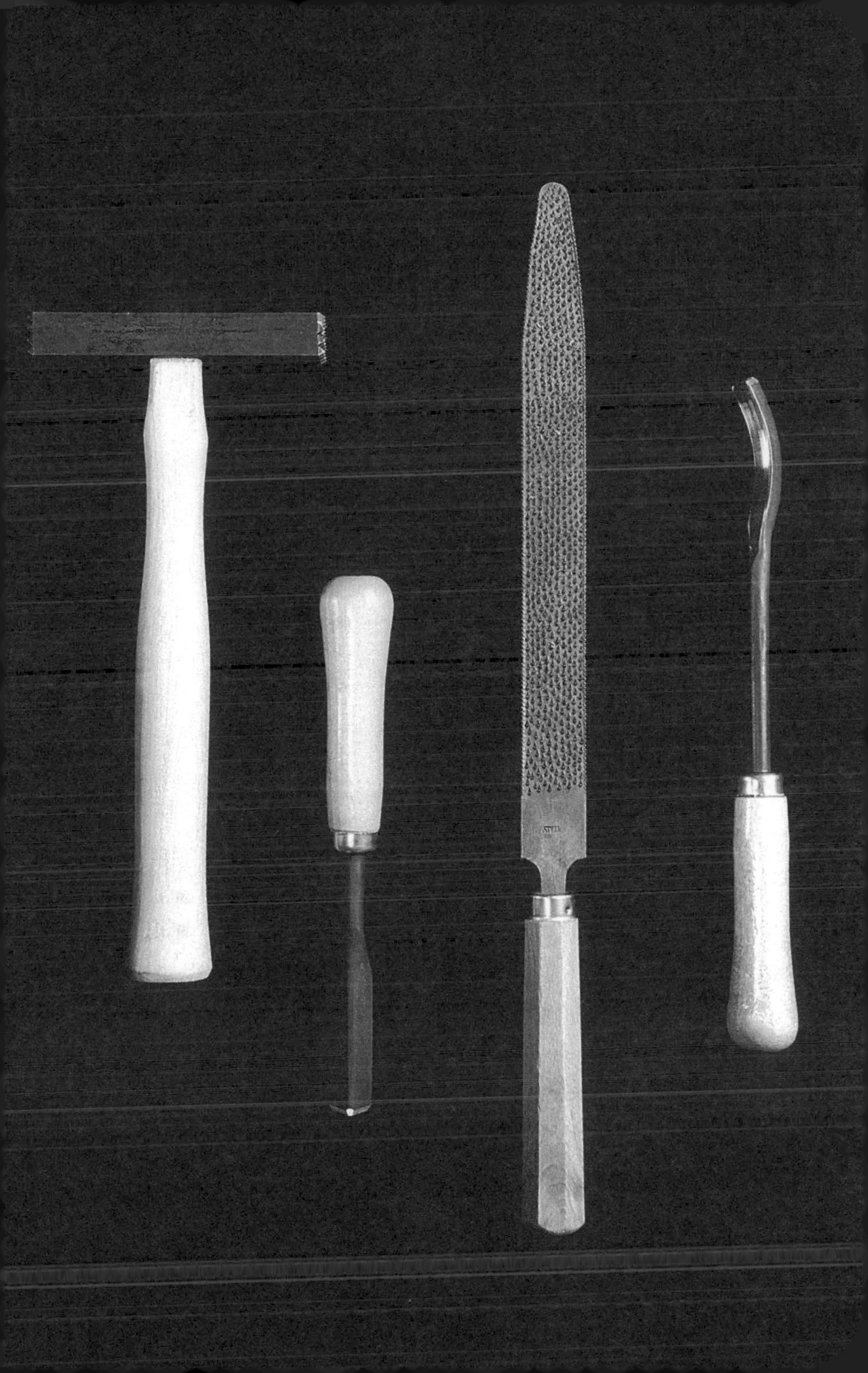

4 affording art

affording aRT

"I felt some nervousness about making my first major art purchase. I was on my first trip to Paris, and I wanted something to mark this important moment. Some people get piercings or tattoos to mark important moments. Some people buy shoes or clothes while in Europe. I felt like buying art, because it's something that I love."
—Arnold

When you're making your gallery rounds, you'll get a feel for the types of dealers and their personalities.

An art gallery serves a couple of functions. It's a showcase for artists open to casual viewers as well as collectors. For the latter group, the gallery is essentially a retail establishment. The dealer who runs the gallery, also known as the gallerist, acts as an advisor, educator, as well as merchant. They're your professional resource and a liaison into the world of art. They can teach you what you need to know—and they are often fascinating, intelligent, sometimes endearingly eccentric people. In your quest to collect, the dealer is a person to trust and enjoy. It's best to choose them wisely, read up on them, and ask around.

There is some truth to the snooty reputation many galleries cultivate, but they're in business to sell like any other business. And if they're really a solid business, they'll also have a workable policy when it comes to returning art that doesn't quite work for you. Like any successful business, a degree of service is a key factor in who rises to the top of the field. If you don't feel comfortable in a gallery, you may not want to do business there. If you're intrigued by the artwork, ask the staff questions about it. Get a sense of how they relate to what's on display.

While museums have art history to answer to, galleries are freer to express particular tastes and biases. After you've seen a few shows at a specific gallery, you'll get a sense of whether it shares your tastes. Dealers usually represent artists exclusively, at least in specific cities. If there's an artist you've come across in a magazine or book, you may have to do a bit of research to find out where their work is available. Modern masters, the Picassos, Matisses and Calders, are often available through various dealers on what's known as the secondary market—meaning the gallery is selling their work for a private collector or the dealer has purchased it from a collector. It's a bit like looking for a classic car with the dealer serving as the clearinghouse. Lesser known artists usually don't enter into the secondary market.

DO YOU LIKE THE ART YOU SEE?

DO YOU FEEL COMFORTABLE IN THE SPACE?

IS THE STAFF FRIENDLY OR HIGH PRESSURE?

IF MONEY WERE NO OBJECT, WHAT PIECE OF ART—FAMOUS OR NOT—WOULD I LOVE TO OWN?

WHAT ABOUT IT MAKES IT SO APPEALING?

Okay, so say you're in a gallery and have found something you love, and maybe want to buy. What next?

First, express your interest to the gallery staff.

They'll be happy to provide you with more information—both aesthetic and financial—that may help you make a decision. At the main desk you'll usually find a binder of material on the artist, which includes a résumé, reviews, and articles. Prices are usually printed on the exhibition checklist. (The cost of an artwork reflects a split between the artist and gallery, usually a 50/50 situation.) Ask about a payment plan—most galleries are happy to sell you an artwork for a set fee per month, though you may have to pay it off before you can bring the art home.

There are a number of factors to consider, so sometimes it's just best to sleep on it. If that piece of art inhabits your dreams as well as your waking hours, chances are you'll regret not doing something about it.

Next comes the art of the transaction. The intersection of art and money is a place of many questions. When value, like beauty, is in the eye of the beholder, how do you know what something is worth? A gallery primarily sets art prices based on artists' reputations—the better known they are, the higher the price may be—but factors such as scale and cost of materials also enter into the picture. For higher-end items, major auctions set the price brackets. If a type of work sells for a certain price on the auction block, figure that's the range you'll be looking at.

The main investment you're making in your collection is in enhancing your life and developing a vision. While artwork may have resale value, that shouldn't be your primary focus as the art market is a fickle place. Ultimately, the economic value of a work of art is whatever you can get the next person to pay for it (which may be more or less than you did). Don't buy art to put your kid through Harvard. Buy art because you love it.

IS THERE ROOM IN MY BUDGET FOR BUYING ART?

I CAN AFFORD TO SPEND ______ PER MONTH ON ARTWORK.

Rental Galleries

Another way to dip your toe in art collecting waters is by working with a rental gallery. Major museums often operate separate galleries that rent out works by local artists for temporary periods of time, and at affordable rates. It's a practice that many businesses use to decorate their offices, but it is also a wonderful way for budding collectors to engage in the process without the pressure of a more final purchase. The practice provides a much-appreciated source of regular income for artists as well.

Go ahead, take home a work of art and see how it feels in your environment.

Chances are you'll come to adore it. Of course, you have the option to buy after the lease ends. (Check with your local museum or municipal art center to see if there's a rental gallery near you.)

Open Studios

While galleries are the primary place to buy art, there are some affordable alternatives, usually a level or two closer to the artists themselves.

In certain situations, you can go directly to the artist. Many artists don't have gallery representation, so they'll make their work visible to the public by opening up their studios, either on their own or as part of an organized group effort. To make the prospect more appealing, buildings with a number of studios and a collective spirit might schedule a weekend event, while some cities have organizations that coordinate larger showcases, in which entire neighborhoods reveal themselves to be teeming with artists.

A primary appeal of visiting an open studio is the opportunity to actually meet the artists and discuss their work, or simply get a sense of where the work is made. Since painting, drawing, or any other art practice is frequently a solitary endeavor, most artists relish the opportunity to meet with interested art viewers. Ask the artists questions; it's not something you can always do in galleries. And you can acquire the work for less, as there's no gallery commission. (You might also ask an artist about a payment plan, though do so gingerly—artists need to make a living like the rest of us.) Mind you, this is a rare opportunity, as once an artist has official gallery representation, it's a no-no to go directly to the source.

You can also begin or build your collection while supporting organizations at benefit auctions.

Benefit Auctions

Most cities have at least one alternative non-profit gallery that serves the needs of local artists by providing a gallery space, as well as a place for people to convene and engage in dialog. As these organizations aren't commercial endeavors, they rely on grants and various other forms of income generation. Quite often an annual art auction is part of the program. Often, other kinds of non-profit organizations—those that address social issues—may turn to the art community to raise money with a benefit auction.

These are very much community-based affairs, and they're festive to boot! A fundraiser is apt to be a party attended by artists who are associated with the gallery, curators, and collectors of varying experience. It's a great place to get a sense of the local scene.

At these events, the art is usually donated by the artists, which means there will be a range of quality and artists' career status represented—well-known figures share the wall space with lesser-knowns. An event like this provides the opportunity to discover young, emerging artists, and to purchase their work at a very affordable price. The risks are minimal. Even if you buy nothing, it's a good opportunity to get a good overview of what's going on in your local art scene.

Preview exhibitions of the artwork usually precede the auctions, often with receptions attached. Scope out the offerings in advance and see what captures your interest. You'll be better prepared for a bidding war, should one arise. There's also plenty of fun to be had by just getting caught up in the frenzy of the auction itself.

The silent auction format is a good introductory method. Rather than having to be vocal in the crowd, the bidding action takes place on sheets of paper, with hopeful buyers marking their bidding price anonymously. Sometimes, the bigger ticket items are relegated to a live auction, with higher rollers going into the ring to fight for a better-known commodity artist.

Auction Houses

After attending one of these events, you may have worked up the gumption to try your hand at the major auction houses—Sotheby's, Christie's, Butterfield's, Phillips and the like.

They're a world unto themselves, with their own rituals and language. A "lot," for example, is a single item or group of items to be sold. At these respected firms, classic, contemporary, and decorative arts (antiques, etc.) are gathered to be auctioned at a specific time. For big sales, the auction houses publish color catalogs of the available works, giving you an opportunity to do your research ahead of time. The items are also available for viewing at preview exhibitions—you'll want to know what you're getting yourself into before raising your auction paddle.

The auction circuit is better suited to conscious acquisitions than to impulse buys. The works range in price (price estimates are printed in the catalogs), so high rollers mingle with normal folk at the actual event. There are, however, ways to engage with the auctions off-site, by submitting absentee bids. All the major auction houses have Internet sites offering pertinent information on live events, as well as online sales. *Art & Auction* magazine is a good resource for the latest news in this exciting arena.

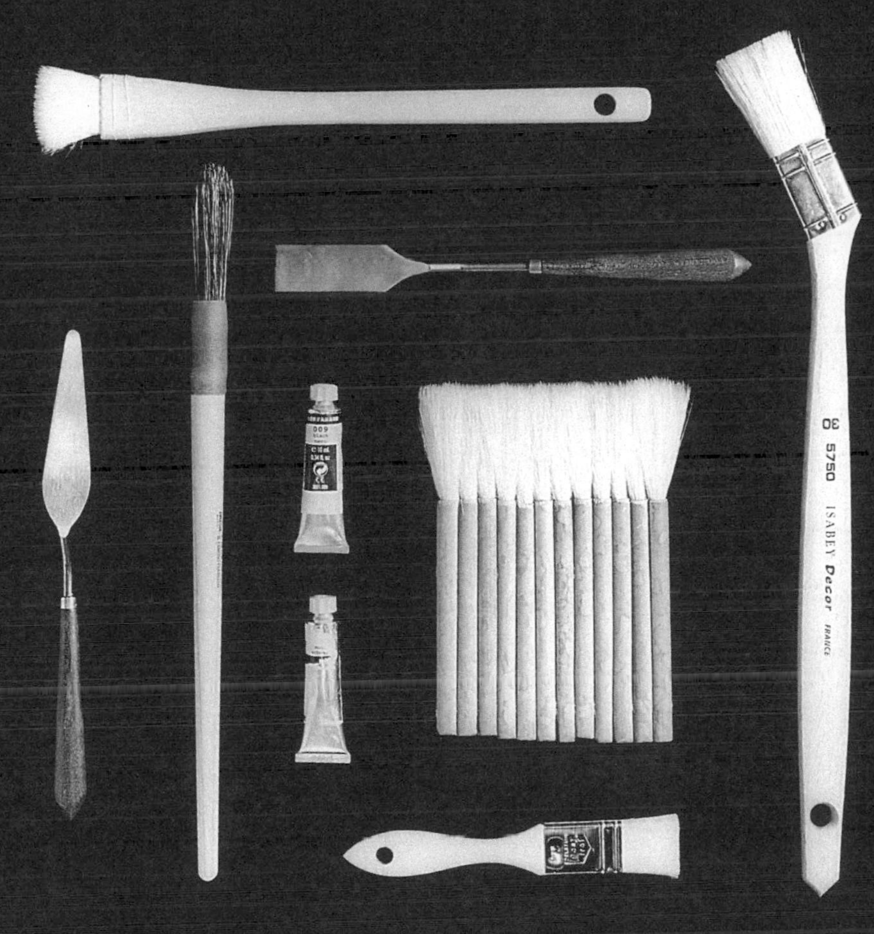
30 5750
ISABEY Decor
FRANCE

caring for art

5

caring for

"I bought a sculpture—a cube of books encased in Plexiglas—that was meant to be hung on the wall. Figuring out where to put it and how to hang it became a whole other part of the art collecting process." —*Molly*

Congratulations! You acquired a work of art! Now what?

There are still a few details to attend to. Each object in your collection is most likely unique or rare. It's a special item that needs to be attended to with special care when it comes to display and maintenance.

Framing

If you're buying a two-dimensional work—a painting, print, drawing, or photograph—you'll most likely want to have it framed.

While the frame fulfills the simple, utilitarian purpose of protecting and showcasing your investment, selecting the most appropriate one is a more complex endeavor than you might expect. The experience, however, has its own pleasures.

There are many aspects to consider when it comes to selecting a frame. And they relate to your own taste as well as enhancing the artwork at hand. You'll need to ask yourself what color should it be? Wood or metal? Thick or thin? Gold-leafed ornate or sleek and simple?

A frame will alter the appearance of the art, so try to select something that maintains the spirit and integrity of the artwork. Then there's the question of having it fit within the style of your décor.

In the case of works on paper or photography, you'll want to select a mat, the visible cardboard that backs and/or creates a window around the piece. You also should consider placing it under glass or Plexiglas, which can be coated with protective UV tints—a guard against the effects of sunlight, which can cause fading. Many prints are on archival paper, which means they are acid free, giving them a longer lifespan.

There's a lot to think about, but contemplating each of these issues will deepen your relationship with the art. Like the process of collecting itself, it's instructive to look at how art is displayed in museums, galleries, and private homes.

You may even grow to appreciate frames in themselves.

"I collect random frames. I aspire to having a wall full of those frames made from turn of the century barns and houses that have been torn down. I collect them and then fill them with my own photographs—memories captured of people, places and moments. I somehow love the idea that they are literally being cradled by a thing that has reinvented a new purpose for itself." —*Kate*

Framing is not inexpensive and it's essential that it be done right. So it's important to find a framer that you trust. Each shop has its own tastes and biases, so get recommendations. Ask your dealer for a suggestion or contact a local museum through their public relations department and find out who frames for them. That way, you know you'll get what's called in the art business 'museum quality' framing. Some commercial framing shops offer quick framing services, which can be functional for something basic. If you're looking for finesse, a custom framer is more appropriate. Some framers specialize in working with a specific medium—old master etchings perhaps. If you're collecting in a specialized arena, keep that in mind.

Bring in your artwork for a consultation; see what the framer suggests. You'll be surprised at the range of options. A quality framer will point out the effects of each possibility, but you'll still have to make the final decision. Again, trust your instincts. You're the one who will be living with it.

A good frame may not come cheaply, but if you care about your art, it's worth the investment. When buying a work of art, look closely at its condition. Scrutinize it; know it really well so that nothing's a surprise when it comes back in a frame.

WHERE HAVE I NOTICED FRAMES IN MUSEUMS, GALLERIES, OR PEOPLE'S HOUSES?

WHAT HAVE I LIKED OR DISLIKED ABOUT THEM?

HOW DO THEY ENHANCE OR DETRACT FROM THE ART?

A piece of art, when
displayed in your home
or office, becomes a part
of a living environment
where real things
happen.

Installing Your Art

The art is framed and chances are you have some idea of where you'd like to put it.

Take the time to select an appropriate location. Consider that a delicately hued watercolor is sensitive to sunlight, while a particular painting may only come alive when illuminated with a pin spotlight. There's even validity to the concern that the painting should look good over the couch—some upholstery shades will complement the art better than others will. Wall colors may also have bearing on how the art will look in your home. Place your new art in the area you're thinking of and see how it works.

Here are a few placement pointers. Generally, you should hang wall art at eye level—so it can be well seen (most people hang their artwork too high). Don't hang delicate works on paper in the bathroom or near the kitchen sink as the proximity to moisture might damage them. Consider your architecture. Drywall may not be able to accommodate a heavy piece—at least not without a special bolt to secure it. Talk to the gallerist or your framer for suggestions.

Hanging and securing a modestly scaled painting on the wall or placing a freestanding sculpture may be a straightforward endeavor (using picture hanging kits available at your local hardware store), but larger more complex works may require a bit of assistance. Galleries work with an installation crew—called preparators—that makes sure the artwork is straight, level, and that nothing will dislodge it from its position. The gallery may refer you to its preparators, but you can also contact a local museum or alternative gallery for other referrals. Sometimes an art-conscious handy person will do. Some works require the artist's hand to be installed optimally, which can be a wonderful way to complete the process of acquisition.

Conservation

Chances are you won't employ a uniformed guard to keep a protective watch while you simply go about your daily life.

On the off chance that an artwork gets damaged—a splash of red wine hits a painting, the cat scratches the woven wall sculpture—what do you do? Don't reach for the tape or Elmer's Glue. It's a job for a professional—that is, an art conservator. Again, your trusted dealer can be of assistance here with a recommendation. If the artist is still living, he or she may be able to make the repair. There are also many private conservators, and they're usually specialists in various media. Some deal only with paintings while others work on textiles.

For a more full-service venue, contact your local museum's conservation department, which often accepts material from outside clients. (It's another way a museum generates income.) In addition to repairing tears or cracks, they may also be able to refresh faded paint colors or remove a dulling layer of age and dirt. Many people don't realize that a good portion of antique or historic art has gone through a bit of a face-lift before being displayed.

Insurance and Appraisal of Artwork

Your art collection is something you will grow to value, so it's important to have it insured.

Any object worth $500 or more should be scheduled on your insurance policy. Standard homeowner's and renter's insurance policies have provisions for this type of addition. Should you begin acquiring a number of works or a very expensive piece, you'll want to take out a separate insurance rider to cover them. While original artwork is a tricky thing to insure as it is impossible to replace it with an identical object should it be lost or stolen, you will still want to protect your investment.

When you purchase a work of art, start a file containing all the relevant papers (invoices, artist biographies, art review, etc.) pertaining to the work. If you buy from a reputable gallery or print publisher, you may even receive a documentation certificate or condition report. Take a snapshot of the work to add to the file. The more comprehensive your records, the more prepared you are should you have to file an insurance claim. If possible, keep a copy of this information in a location other than your home.

For a few items, the insurance solution outlined above is sufficient. But as your art collection grows, you may want to consider having a formal appraisal done. Before doing so, it is important that you locate an accredited appraiser through an official organization. There are three major associations with international and national chapters. They are self-regulated and set standards for the industry. They are:

THE AMERICAN SOCIETY OF APPRAISERS

THE APPRAISAL ASSOCIATION OF AMERICA

THE INTERNATIONAL SOCIETY OF APPRAISERS

An appraiser will evaluate for insurance purposes, one item or as many as are in your collection. An appraiser can examine other items of value in your home—a silver tea service, Oriental rug, antique clock—and add them to your insurance appraisal. The appraiser will examine your work of art either by looking at a photograph or making a physical inspection, depending on the work in question. He or she will assess the value of your works based on their current replacement value—that is what it would cost you to buy a piece similar in size, quality, and subject matter in the current market.

We're focusing on insurance appraisals here, but appraisals are also required when art is donated to institutions (should you choose to part with your art) or is part of an estate for future activity. The appraisal will provide a description of the objects and their condition, their provenance (a list of prior owners and exhibition venues), and details of their acquisition. The appraisal will also include a photo of the work and any relevant documentation together with the appraiser's qualifications. Some online sites offer appraisals at a starting price of $25.

This may seem like yet another domestic task to be bothered with, but insuring your beloved acquisition is definitely worth your while. Should you be hit with theft, fire, flood, or other unthinkable disasters, your insured work of art stands a far better chance of being restored or replaced with far less hassle than its uninsured counterpart.

A complete appraisal will state the purpose of the appraisal and its intended use.

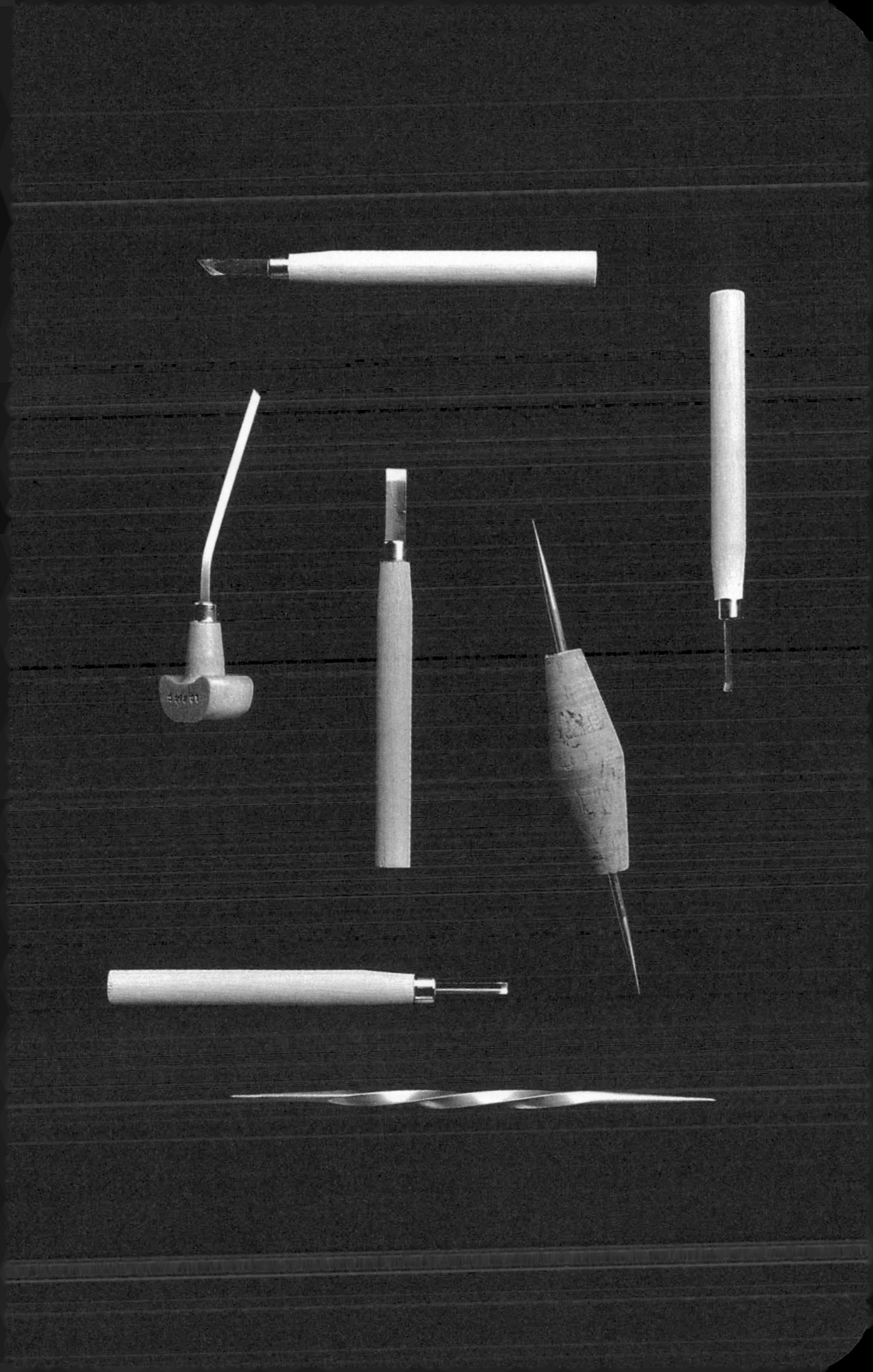

you've got art

6

you've got

aRT

Congratulations! You've got art.

It's in your life, and chances are it feels pretty good. You've now entered into a new world, which will get more meaningful and fulfilling the longer you engage with it.

Use the following space to record the evolution and growth of your collection. Start at the beginning:

THE FIRST PIECE OF ART I BOUGHT

Artist's name:

Title:

Medium:

Date it was made:

When I bought it:

Where I bought it:

How much I paid for it:

Things about it that made me want it:

Memories and anecdotes I associate with the piece:

THE NEXT PIECES

Artist's name:

Title:

Medium:

Date it was made:

When I bought it:

Where I bought it:

How much I paid for it:

Things about it that made me want it:

Memories and anecdotes I associate with the piece:

Artist's name:

Title:

Medium:

Date it was made:

When I bought it:

Where I bought it:

How much I paid for it:

Things about it that made me want it:

Memories and anecdotes I associate with the piece:

Artist's name:

Title:

Medium:

Date it was made:

When I bought it:

Where I bought it:

How much I paid for it:

Things about it that made me want it:

Memories and anecdotes I associate with the piece:

Artist's name:

Title:

Medium:

Date it was made:

When I bought it:

Where I bought it:

How much I paid for it:

Things about it that made me want it:

Memories and anecdotes I associate with the piece:

Artist's name:

Title:

Medium:

Date it was made:

When I bought it:

Where I bought it:

How much I paid for it:

Things about it that made me want it:

Memories and anecdotes I associate with the piece:

"Sometimes I look around my house and I'll count how many pieces of art I have. It amazes me that I have as much as I do—and it's all kinds of stuff I've gotten in a variety of ways. I never imagined that I would have a 'collection'. I'm actually getting to the point where I have more art than I have room to display. It's not like I'll be building my own museum any time soon, but the whole range of things does seem like part of my legacy. I love that." —*Jean*

FALCON
MINIATURE
UTILITY MFG. CO.
NEW YORK
BROWNIE Holiday Flash CAMERA
INSTAMATIC 100

RESOURCES

BOOKS: A by no means comprehensive list of books on the subject of art history, art collecting, and art appreciation.

History of Art

Atkins, Robert. *ArtSpeak: A Guide to Contemporary Ideas, Movements, and Buzzwords, 1945 to the Present.* New York: Abbeville Press, 1997.

————————. *ArtSpoke: A Guide to Modern Ideas, Movements, and Buzzwords, 1848-1944*. New York: Abbeville Press, 1993.

Chipp, Herschel. *Theories of Modern Art.* Berkeley: University of California Press, 1989.

Gombrich, Ernst. *The Story of Art.* New York: Phaidon Press, Inc., 1995.

Janson, H. W. and Anthony F. Janson. *History of Art,* 6th ed. New York: Prentice Hall, 2000.

Kleiner, Fred S., Christin J. Mamiya and Richard G. Tansey. *Gardner's Art Through The Ages.* New York: Harcourt, 2001.

Langmuir, Erika and Norbert Lynton. *Yale Dictionary of Art and Artists.* New Haven: Yale University Press, 2000.

Murray, Peter and Linda Lefevre. *Penguin Dictionary of Art and Artists.* New York: Penguin USA, 1992.

Schmied, Wieland, Frank Whitford and Frank Zoellner. *The Prestel Dictionary of Art and Artists in the 20th Century.* New York: Prestel USA, 2000.

The 20th Century Art Book. New York: Phaidon Press, 1996.

Collecting and Caring for Art

Austin-Smith, Vicki and Werner L. Muensterberger. *Collecting: An Unruly Passion.* New York: Harvest Books, 1995.

Brown, Jay. *The Complete Guide to Art Prints: How to Identify, Invest & Care for Your Collection.* Iola, WI: Krause Publications, 1999.

Frank, Jeanne. *Discovering Art: A User's Guide to the World of Collecting.* New York: Thunder's Mouth Press, 1997.

Guggenheim, Peggy. *Out of This Century: Confessions of an Art Addict.* New York: Universe Books, 1979.

Maciolek, Cindi R. *The Basics of Buying Art.* Las Vegas: Grand Arbor Press, 1998.

Schultz, Arthur W., ed. *Caring for Your Collections.* New York: Harry N. Abrams, 1992.

Vartian, Armen R. *Legal Guide to Buying and Selling Art and Collectibles.* Chicago: Bonus Books, 1997.

Looking at and Appreciating Art

Acton, Mary. *Learning to Look at Paintings.* New York: Routledge, 1997.

Arnheim, Rudolf. *Visual Thinking.* Berkeley: University of California Press, 1989.

Berger, John. *Ways of Seeing.* New York: Viking, 1995.

——————— *About Looking.* New York: Vintage, 1992.

Elkins, James. *How to Use Your Eyes.* New York: Routledge, 2000.

Ellis, Estelle, et al. *At Home with Art: How Art Lovers Live with and Care for Their Treasures.* New York: Clarkson Potter, 1999.

Hickey, Dave. *Air Guitar: Essays on Art & Democracy.* New York: Distributed Art Publishers, 1997.

Hughes, Robert. *American Visions: The Epic History of Art in America.* New York: Knopf, 1997.

———————. *The Shock of the New.* New York: Knopf, 1991.

FAVORITE ART BOOKS:

PERIODICALS: A selection of periodicals covering the art world, most with an emphasis on modern and contemporary art. The most popular of these magazines, *Art in America*, *Artforum*, and *ARTnews*, are often available at general newsstands or bookstores. Some of the others you might need to go hunting for at museum shops or specialty stores.

American Painter—A specialty publication focusing on painters and painting in the U.S.A.

Art in America—One of the three biggies (with *ArtNews* and *Artforum*), it includes essays, news, and reviews on contemporary and historical art.

Art and Antiques—As the title implies, a source for stories and information on collecting—both art and antiques. Articles on artists and art issues round things out.

Art and Auction—Subtitled "Inside the Art Market," this publication offers the inside scoop on the latest auction activities, market trends, and their effect on art itself.

Art Issues—Art as it's made and perceived in Los Angeles is the focus here, with essays, color portfolios, and reviews.

Art Newspaper—Published eleven times a year, this British magazine is the paper of record when it comes to accurate art news reporting.

Art on Paper—A publication of news, features, and reviews focused not just on drawings, but on photography, prints, and mixed media works.

Artbyte—This magazine of digital culture concentrates on the social and artistic implications of new technologies as they relate to visual art, design, film, and lifestyle.

Artforum—Discussing art along with fashion, film, books, and technology gives this intellectually bent, sometimes jargon-laden monthly, a cutting edge.

ARTnews—Of the three most popular American art publications, this is the *Time* of the bunch. It devotes a hefty percentage of ink to artist, museum, and collector news along with features and exhibition reviews.

Art/Text—This well-designed journal, published out of Australia and Los Angeles, features scholarly yet pop essays, features and reviews of contemporary art seen and made in the Pacific Rim.

Flash Art—The contemporary international art scene is covered through essays, news, and reviews in this glossy magazine published in Milan.

Gallery Guide—Listings of gallery schedules, maps, and short previews of exhibitions. It's a basic guide to art near you.

Modern Painters—Slick yet stately, this British publication offers essays and reviews that consciously veer away from pretentious art language. And David Bowie's on the editorial board.

Sculpture—Three-dimensional art, not surprisingly, is the focus here, with an emphasis on aesthetic issues.

Smock—The fashion world meets the art world in this hip publication, which leans heavily on the side of lifestyle and design.

WEB SITES: There is a limitless array of information about art, artists, collecting, galleries, and museums available online. Here are some useful sites to get you started in your search.

For Buying Art
www.artMecca.com

www.artnet.com

www.eyestorm.com

www.guild.com

www.nextmonet.com

www.onview.com

For Appraising Art
The American Society of Appraisers
www.appraisers.org

The Appraisers Association of America
www.appraisersassoc.org

The International Society of Appraisers
www.isa-appraisers.org

For Finding Art to Look At

Art Museum Network
www.amn.org

Artcyclopedia.com
www.artcyclopedia.com

Gallery Guide Online
www.galleryguide.org

Museum Network.com
www.museumnetwork.com

For Looking at Art

The Museum of Modern Art, New York
www.moma.org

The Metropolitan Museum of Art, New York
www.metmuseum.org

High Museum of Art, Atlanta, GA
www.high.org

The Brooklyn Museum
www.brooklynart.org

The Art Institute of Chicago
www.artic.org

The San Francisco Museum of Modern Art
www.sfmoma.org

The Los Angeles County Museum of Art
www.lacma.org

The Museum of Contemporary Art, Los Angeles, CA
www.moca-la.org

The Menil Collection, Houston, TX
www.menil.org

The Nelson-Atkins Museum of Art, Kansas City, Missouri
www.nelson-atkins.org

The New Museum of Contemporary Art, New York, NY
www.newmuseum.org

The Philadelphia Museum of Art
www.philamuseum.org

The Seattle Museum of Art
www.seattleartmuseum.org

The Tate Modern, London
www.tate.org.uk/modern

Van Gogh Museum, Amsterdam, Holland
www.vangoghmuseum.nl/ehp.html

The Wadsworth Athenaeum
www.wadsworthatheneum.org

FAVORITE WEB SITES:

PERSONAL RESOURCES

FAVORITE MUSEUMS:

FAVORITE COMMERCIAL GALLERIES:

FAVORITE NON-PROFIT/ALTERNATIVE GALLERIES:

OPEN STUDIO EVENTS:

NEARBY ART SCHOOLS (OFFERING CLASSES, LECTURES, AND EXHIBITIONS):

NAMES AND NUMBERS OF FRAMERS:

NOTES ON THE FRAMER'S ADVICE:

NAMES AND NUMBERS OF ART PREPARATORS:

NAMES AND NUMBERS OF CONSERVATORS:

NAMES AND NUMBERS OF INSURANCE AGENTS AND APPRAISERS: